I WANT TO BE A
NUTRITIONIST

Written by
Jonathan Reule

Illustration
Christiane Tee

First paperback edition October 2023
ISBN 978-981-18-6530-5

Published by Unibino Pte. Ltd.
9 North Buona Vista Drive, #02-01 Metropolis Tower 1, Singapore 138588

www.unibino.com

If you think back to how we lived in the long ago past, you'd probably imagine a very different lifestyle than today. In prehistoric times, humans didn't have the choice of whether they wanted to be in shape or not. We had to use our strength to catch our food, build our homes, and sometimes travel far distances on foot!

But as we evolved and learned to better provide for ourselves, we started to place more emphasis on farming - so we might have more food to last us through the winters. Also, hunting used up more energy and gave us less of a reward in the long run.

So, as we progressed, we focused on enhancing our situation by inventing convenient tools for farming and crop transportation.

Soon, we industrialised our cities. That way, we no longer needed to fret over wild animals attacking our villages. Which made our daily toils less of a burden.

This, of course, has led us to the modernised cities of today. Where technology allows us to do things our ancestors never could've imagined. We can order food from our phones, live in giant skyscrapers, work late into the night with modern lighting, and several other things that were unthought of in the past.

Yet this sense of progress has come at a cost. With more food available and less need to work outdoors for meals, our lives have become sedentary.

What's worse, modern food, with its convenience, has also come with another hefty price tag. That is its lack of nutritional value.

Modern meals often include fast-food burgers full of additives, pizzas loaded with grease, and deep-fried chicken covered in oil!

Unfortunately, the effects of poor nutrition have impacted not only adults but children too. Obesity is more common now than it has ever been in the entire span of human history.

This has led to overcrowded hospitals with a sharp increase in visits from the average population.

But thankfully, this is where our nutritionists come in handy. You see, these professionals have created a career out of helping people to achieve optimal health conditions.

LOVE YOURSELF LIVE HEALTHY
HEALTHY LIV[ING]
thank you!
Luis Diallo
FOOD

Now, you may be asking, how do nutritionists help people achieve their best health standards? It all starts with a basic assessment. They'll find out your weight, height, diet, and how often you exercise.

With this information, they will be able to gauge your level of health and determine a plan of action to get you into shape!

If overweight, a nutritionist might suggest an exercise regimen along with a more balanced diet with plenty of low-fat options.

It is usually the patient who keeps track of their progress on a daily basis.

This is normally done with a special food and exercise journal.

Don't fret though - the nutritionist will also conduct periodical evaluations and tailor additional recommendations to help you make the best progress possible.

It's a common misconception that only overweight individuals need to visit a nutritionist. This is far from the case, as many lifestyle diseases can arise no matter a person's shape or size. High blood pressure, diabetes, and even hypertension can be common ailments.

Next, you may be wondering what it takes to become a nutritionist.

Well, first, there are several different types of nutritionists and choosing the right fit will be a great start!

There are four main branches of nutritionists.

Oncological,
and Paediatric.

Holistic nutritionists are known for incorporating alternative techniques in their work compared to typical practices. Many not only focus on natural foods and exercise but also talk with clients about their emotional health.

Sports nutritionists, on the other hand, work alongside athletes, helping them to create appropriate diets, exercise routines, and plans to help their bodies recover as fast as possible from their rigorous training sessions.

Pediatric nutritionists help children with genetic and lifestyle diseases while working closely with their parents to help incorporate any necessary changes.

Whereas Oncological nutritionists make exercise and lifestyle plans for cancer patients who need special care while they undergo regular hospital treatments.

Most places in the world require nutritionists to have a degree related to health before becoming certified in the field. That's why many consider a degree in health sciences or other specialised areas of study.

But there are still places where you can attend a course focusing on holistic nutrition without going to university. Yet, one thing that all nutritionists are required to take part in is a certificate program before starting to practice on their own.

This program will start after you have a degree in a related field, where you will work under a certified nutritionist, gaining enough supervised clinical hours before you are given a final exam to obtain your certificate.

After receiving the proper certification, it's up to you to decide where you'll work.

Depending on your specialisation, you could have a whole variety
of workplaces to choose from. Nutritionists can be found all over

from hospitals,

to community care groups,

to sports teams,

to their own private clinics.

No matter which route you may choose, know that being a nutritionist is a great profession that helps many clients along the way.

Although we are living in a world very different from our ancestors, it is still important that we try our best to take care of ourselves.

In this sense, what are some ways you start leading a healthy lifestyle from today? Perhaps there are already several things you are doing that keep you in good shape, but other areas you'd like to change?

Now that you know what a nutritionist does, it's up to you to decide if this might be the right career for you. Because no matter which branch you decide upon, being a nutritionist is a great way to interact with others, and help make this world a better place.

MY HEALTH
JOURNAL

My Inspiration

Shubhi Saxena
Founder, Unibino

As a parent in this ever-changing world, it can sometimes feel overwhelming when it comes to our children's futures. New technologies seem to be arising almost every day, and with so many innovations, it creates unique professions which many of us wouldn't have dreamed to be necessary only a few years ago. Which to me is a good thing. Because with so much variety, my children can have the opportunity to pick a career that will fit their personalities and build upon their strengths. As you may imagine, this desire within me to provide my children with the resources they needed to thrive, led me to search out books that would be easy enough for them to understand while teaching them about various professions.

Only, I found that these books were few and far between. Even if I could find a book about a certain profession geared towards young readers, I found them sparse inside and limited to only certain careers that may not fit my children's abilities. This is when I came up with the idea to write my own children's books, teaching them about all the various careers in the modern world. After months of researching different professions and learning more than I ever expected, I quickly realised this was going to be a bigger project than I first anticipated. I dove into the histories of these professions, discovering links to the past, and why these professions were now so important.

Ultimately my goal was to offer my children options, to show them that there is no one set path for everyone. But in this, I stumbled upon something bigger. I wanted to share this with future generations. To share with all children and parents about these careers, to help spark curiosity, and to instil a passion for the future. Everyone has special talents and abilities, and I hope that this series will be able to offer clarity and inspiration to children around the world. Because at the end of the day, it's never too early to start dreaming and never too late to take action. With this, I hope you enjoy this series and that your young ones become the best versions of themselves as they can achieve.

9 789811 865305